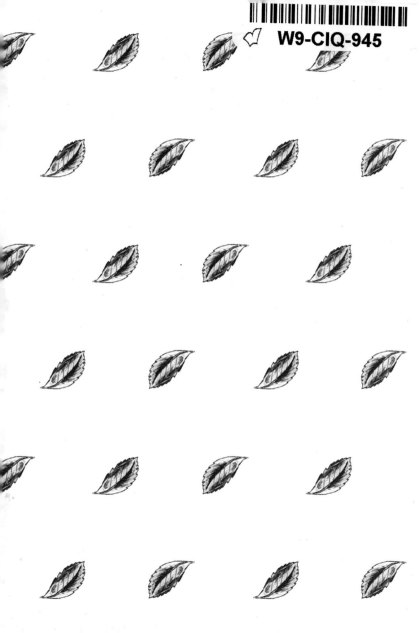

" *Mate is in use in every house all day long, and the compliment of the country is to hand the mate-cup to every visitor, the same cup and tube serving for all, and an attendant being kept in waiting to replenish for each person.*

Throughout the provinces, the weary traveller, let him stop at what hovel soever he may, is sure to be presented with the hospitable mate-cup, which, unless his prejudices are very strong indeed, will be found a great refreshment. "

Emeric Essex Vidal, 1820

This book was written with the help of the following people:
Ana Rosa Argibay Molina de Goyeneche who kindly helped me with the English translation.
Nené Weil whose enthusiasm, knowledge and library are inexhaustible.
My brother Carlos who lent me all the books of all travellers who visited this blessed land.

Other books published by Maizal

Español/Spanish
El Tango
El Gaucho
Argentina Natural
La Cocina Argentina
Vinos Argentinos
Carne Argentina
Indígenas Argentinos
El Mate

Inglés/English
The Tango
The Gaucho
Argentine Nature
Argentine Cookery
Argentine Wines
Argentine Beef
Argentine Indians

Bilingüe/Bilingual
Teatro Colón
Pintura Argentina/
Argentine Painting

Argentrip
Argentina's on-line travel guide
www.argentrip.com

Book and Cover Design: Christian le Comte and Sophie le Comte
© Mónica G. Hoss de le Comte, 1999
Hecho el depósito que previene la ley 11.723
ISBN 987-97899-0-3
Published by Maizal
Muñiz 438, B1640FDB, Martinez
Buenos Aires, Argentina.
E-mail: maizal@argentrip.com
Printed in September 2003 by Morgan International.

Mónica Gloria Hoss de le Comte

The Mate

The Mate Ceremony

"We gathered round the camp-fire and the mate started making its visits." Ricardo Güiraldes, Don Segundo Sombra, 1926

When people gather to drink mate something magical happens. It is a simple, humble, daily custom and yet it has all the characteristics of a ceremony. Like any other ceremony it has its rites which have to be  carefully performed in the same way, day after day.

It is a moment of leisure with friends and family. In the country, the *gauchos* sit together around the *fogón* (the camp-fire), sipping their mate after a long day's work.

Tiredness breeds silence and silently the mate circles from hand to hand. And then, slowly, conversation starts, people come closer together, confidences are exchanged.

The mate ceremony resembles the American rite of the calumet, the pipe of peace. There, too, the pipe goes from hand to hand, completing the circle, offering hospitality and goodwill.

Mate is drunk by almost everybody: it is drunk by the trucker and his companion in the loneliness of the long, never-ending routes (they use a vessel with a wide mouth into which it is easy to pour the hot water in spite of the jolts along the track); by students, when studying; by workers during their midday rest; at home for breakfast or on any other occasion, rain or shine, in summer or in winter.

The Word "Mate"
The Guaraní Indians, who live in the northern part of Argentina and the south of Paraguay and who taught the Spanish conquerors to drink mate, call the gourd – the vessel from which mate is drunk – caáiguá. The Quechua Indians (who live in what is today Bolivia, Peru and northern Argentina) call it "mati". The Spaniards adopted this word to call not only the vessel but also the tea-like beverage which is prepared with yerba, the dried leaves of an evergreen tree found in that region which was called "caá" by the Indians.

*J. L. Pallière
(1823-1887)
Interior of a Rancho*

The Plant

Yerba mate (*Ilex paraguayensis*) belongs to the family of the Aquifoliaceae (the holly family). It is an evergreen tree which normally grows up to 8 or 10 meters. Its grey trunk is short and smooth, and its multistemmed crown is dark green.

Its flowers are small and white and they bloom from September to December.

The leaves have indented margins and the young leaves and terminal buds are collected and used as raw material for the production of *yerba*. The tree grows wild in an exuberant region of Argentina, Paraguay and the South of Brasil.

It needs fertile soil and a subtropical climate: humidity and the heat of the burning sun. Several attempts have been made to grow *yerba* in Asia or Africa but they were unsuccessful. The present of the good Tupá was only for the Guaraní jungle.

When planted, the seed does not grow spontaneously because its coating is very hard and does not disintegrate in the soil. Aimé Bonpland (1773-1858), the famous French doctor and botanist, who arrived in Buenos Aires in 1817, was obsessed with the problem. How could the plant grow wild? The Jesuits knew how to cultivate mate, but they had taken the secret with them when they were forced to leave the country. The seeds need the acid digestive juices of the birds to germinate. The seeds fall from heaven without the seed-coat after the birds have eaten the fruits from the *yerba* tree. Bonpland had not read Florian Paucke, the German Jesuit who vividly explains the methodology used in the missions of the Mocobí indians in the mid eighteenth century. In his report "To and Fro" he says: "Nobody can imagine the utility of this bird [a toucan]. These birds plant the herb drunk by the Paraguayans...they eat the seeds of the herb which are then evacuated through the natural exit."

The American traveller H. M. Brackenridge in his *Voyage to Buenos Aires* in the years 1817 and 1818 wrote: "The quantities of this herb consumed in the viceroyalty of La Plata, and exported to Chili and Peru, was, at one time, very great; but the interruption of their trade, occasioned by the revolution, and the restrictive system adopted by the government of Paraguay has occasioned it to diminish. Its use is said to have been borrowed from the Indians, with whom it had been known time immemorial. It is a large shrub, which grows wild throughout Paraguay, and on the east side of the Paraná... It is stated never to have been cultivated, and has not been accurately described by botanists."

Alexander Caldleugh in his *Travels in South America, During the Years 1819-1821* writes: "... on leaving the country, I missed it [mate] exceedingly ... None of the seeds, which are like black pepper, which I brought over, have come up; but it is believed that, ultimately, the plant will be cultivated with success in England. De Termeyer, who resided some years among the Guaranis, says, he could not succeed in raising it in Italy on his return ... The usual mode of judging of its goodness is, by placing a little on the

Tupá's Present
Once upon a time a tired and hungry stranger reached the house of an old man who lived with his daughter in the Guaraní jungle. Although the old man was very poor, he gave the stranger shelter and shared with him his scanty meal.
The stranger, who turned out to be Tupá, the good God of the Guaraní Indians, left the tree of the yerba mate as a present. Today the Indians still pary to Caá Yará, the Lord of the Yerba, that they will never lack their miraculous plant.

Illustrations
J. Sánchez
Labrador, S. J.
(1717-1798)

P. Montenegro, S. J.
(1663-1728)

F. Paucke, S. J.
(1719-1779)

palm of the hand and blowing it; when, if none remains, it is considered old and devoid of flavour... It certainly possesses excellent stomachic qualities."

Illustration
F. Paucke, S. J.
(1719-1779)

Univers Pittoresque
(1840)

J. M. Blanes
(1830-1901)
Drinking Mate

Manufacturing Yerba

The first step in the preparation of *yerba* is called *sapecado*: the leafy branches are put to dry by means of a fire kindled around the leaves. This preliminary roasting will inhibit the enzymes that produce fermentation and prevent the leaves from oxidizing and losing their green colour.

Immediately after this process, the leaves are dried in a current of dry air.

Yerba is then ground into a coarse mixture (the process is called *cancheo*) and then packed in bags and left to rest for 9 months.

During this time the flavour is heightened and *yerba* acquires its characteristic bouquet. Then the dry leaves are crushed and mixed with other leaves to get the right blend.

There are two sorts of mixtures, the *caá-guazú* (big sort) in which the *yerba* leaves are ground together with small pieces of branches or the finer mixture called *caá-mini*, (small sort), where the branches are left out. The latter is considered to be of superior quality.

The busiest time in the plantations is between May and October, the time of the year, when *yerba* is harvested. For this activity the branches are cut with a long knife called a machete.

The Story of Mate

"Yerba is one of the enchantments of this land",
Nicolás Mastrilli Durán, S. J. Annual letter, 1628.

Father Florian Paucke says that the most distinguished Spanish families used to discard the first mate brewed, it was usually drunk by the servant. The reason for this was that the yerba leaves were often intermingled with powder and sand. Today the first mate is drunk by the cebador, *the person in charge of preparing mate.*

The Indians drank the infusion made from the leaves of Caá directly from an earthenware pot without using the *bombilla* (a long tube with a strainer at one end). They filtered the drink with their teeth, spitting the leaves out from their mouths, or they sucked the mate through a cane.

During their long walks through the jungle the Indians used to munch the leaves as well, but this custom has disappeared nowadays. Harvesting and carrying *yerba* from the jungle was hard work because the Indians had to cross marshy regions with their heavy loads.

The Spaniards adopted *mate* almost immediately and they called the leaves "Herb from Paraguay" not knowing that the plant was a tree. At the end of the

PARAQVARIA
Vulgo
PARAGVAY.
Cum adjacentibus.

sixteenth century the first Jesuits arrived. Their mission was to evangelize the Indians. At the beginning they considered mate drinking a dangerous habit so much so that they even presented it as a case before the Tribunal of the Holy Inquisition in Lima in 1610. Later on mate was accepted, and the Jesuits even encouraged its use as a solution to the problem of drunkenness. The Indians used to get drunk on *chicha* which is a highly alcoholic drink obtained from the fermentation of the fruit of a tree called *algarrobo* (carob tree).

The Jesuits started cultivating *yerba mate* near the missions after having got permission to trade in it in 1645. It became their most important source of income and they were able to pay the tribute to His Catholic Majesty with the revenue.

In the mid eighteenth century mate was drunk by all social classes. When it started being drunk in Buenos Aires each family has a special servant who was in charge of brewing mate, sometimes even two, one for sweet mate and another one for the mate served plain (*cimarrón*).

When Charles III signed in 1767 the Expulsion Act and the Jesuits had to leave the country, the settlements in the missions were slowly deserted and the plantations were lost so that *yerba* had to be harvested in the jungle again, where it grows wild. At the beginning of the twentieth century, the first commercial crops were cultivated in the same place where the Jesuits had had theirs. Today there are 130.000 hectares under cultivation. Bolivia, Chile and Peru, and in particular, Argentina, Brazil, Paraguay and Uruguay are mate consumers. From the Indians in the Pampa to the European immigrants, all have adopted the beverage. Today it is considered the national drink.

Aimé Bompland by C. E. Pellegrini (1800-1875)

Although the expedition of Louis A. de Bougainville (1729-1814) took samples of yerba to Europe in 1764, nobody cared about yerba until 1818 when Aimé Bompland studied the possibility of its cultivation.

Illustration Map of Paraguay (1635)

"Curing" the Mate

"Fragrant, like a cured mate, the night…"
Jorge Luis Borges, Fervor de Buenos Aires, Caminata, 1923.

**J. M. Rugendas
(1802-1858)
Gauchos**

The dried hollow gourd from the *Lagenaria Vulgaris* which is used as a vessel for brewing mate has to be "cured" before using it for the first time. To cure a mate one has to fill the gourd (mate) with leaves of used *yerba*, add a jet of hot water and leave the *yerba* to macerate.

After 24 hours, the leaves are discarded and with the help of a spoon the remaining flesh in the gourd, which should be soft and flabby by this time, is scraped off. This process has to be repeated twice so as to clean the mate completely.

The Mate

The mate most commonly used, is a gourd of the *Lagenaria Vulgaris*, a climbing plant, which grows in the same region as *yerba mate*. The gourd is put to dry and hollowed out. It can have several forms; *poro*, which has the form of a pear; *galleta*, which means cracker because it is flat and round. The *poro* is used for sweet mate, the *galleta* for *cimarrón*.

In order to identify their own mate, the Indians and then the Spaniards started carving their names on it or they painted the mate. They also covered the mate with leather to protect it, especially in those provinces where it was difficult to get a gourd.

When the mate became a luxury good, the silversmiths started ornamenting it with all sorts of decorations. The whole vessel was then made of silver, keeping the form of the original gourd. Since the mate cannot always stand by itself, the silversmiths created beautiful bases for them.

Old mates are rare and sought by collectors are after them, especially those mates made of silver, but the genuine mate drinker prefers his gourd to a silver mate because he says that a well "cured" mate contributes to the good taste of his drink.

Wooden mate

"During the evening, I had the opportunity, for the first time, of seeing and tasting the herb of Paraguay, or mate, as prepared by these people. It is called mate, from the name of the vessel; usually a small gourd, by the poorer sort, or silver, and even wood (nearly of the same shape) cased with copper for the rich. About a handful of the bruised

Guaraní gourd

Paraguayan Mate

Peruvian Mate

leaves of the *yerba*, intermingled with small twigs, for it is not prepared with the cleanliness and care of the East India tea, is put into three half-gills of warm water; the mate, itself, holding about a pint. As it is used, the water is occasionally renewed, and in taking it, they use a tube a few inches in length, with a perforated bulb at the end, as a strainer. Sugar is sometimes added to it. The taste is an agreeable bitter, and bears some resemblance to the Chinese tea. It does not form a part of a social meal, nor is anything eaten with it; it is taken just as inclination prompts, at all times of the day, though more generally in the morning and evening, or after having undergone some bodily fatigue. The decoction possesses, according to them, exhilarating and restorative qualities. As there were not mates enough for each, I saw them, without repugnance, using the same after each other; but I afterwards observed, that this was not the case in the more refined portions of society." *Voyage to Buenos Aires, (performed in the years 1817 and 1818, by orders of the American Government),* by H. M. Brackenridge.

Chilean Mate

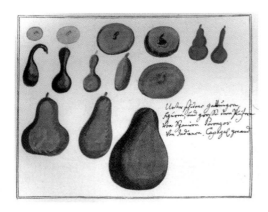

The Bombilla

"In its crudest form the *bombilla* is a reed or thin joint of bamboo, over the lower end of which a few horse-hairs have been woven, or a small bit of loose cloth has been tied.

In its more advanced and mechanically perfect form it is a tube closed at the lower end except for a number of small perforations.

Its latest development is the product of the art of the silversmith, and consists of a tube, which has at the bottom a spoon-like expansion, covered with a little lid, which is perforated by numerous small openings." This is the accurate report of an American traveller, W. J. Holland, in his book *To the River Plate and Back*, 1913.

The silver *bombillas* are elaborately ornamented with figures of plants and birds. The most curious *bombillas* are the curved ones, used to drink mate in bed. The ultimate feeling of happiness and satisfaction.

John Miers, in *Travels in Chile and La Plata*, 1826, says "Awakening just before the dawn of day, a curious picturesque scene presented itself. Part of the family had risen and having lighted a fire under the triangle, as many as could edge in were huddled round it; some were seated on small blocks of wood; others on their heels with their knees in their faces; the blazing fire cast a strong light, which, contrasted with the deep shade of the black ground, displayed the whole group, their rude dresses and strange postures; the effect was singular and remarkable. They were in earnest conversation, and the *matecito* was handed round from one to another, each his turn taking a sip through the long tin tube of the infusion of *yerba*, out of the little calabash, or *matecito*."

"The whole scene and circumstances of the time led me almost to imagine that we were bivouacking among the Indians, or among some of the savage outcasts of society."
John Miers

Illustrations
F. Paucke, S. J.
(1719-1779)

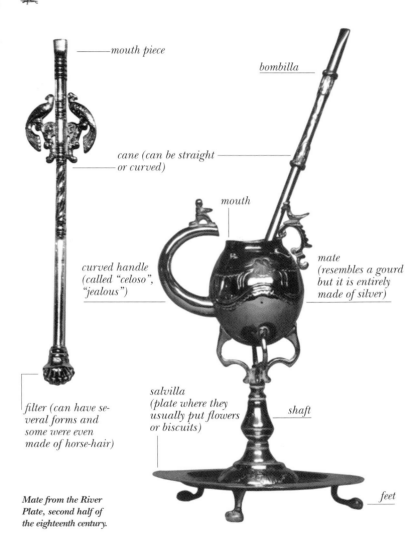

mouth piece

bombilla

cane (can be straight or curved)

mouth

curved handle (called "celoso", "jealous")

mate (resembles a gourd but it is entirely made of silver)

filter (can have several forms and some were even made of horse-hair)

salvilla (plate where they usually put flowers or biscuits)

shaft

feet

Mate from the River Plate, second half of the eighteenth century.

The Yerbera

A *yerbera* is the vessel where the supply of *yerba* for daily use is kept. It is usually divided into two receptacles, one for *yerba* and the other one for sugar.
A long spoon is kept in the *yerbera*, used to fill the mate – the gourd – with *yerba*.

Chilean Mate (with "trembleques", tremblers. These ornaments tremble when one holds the mate)

The Pava Hornillo

Pava means kettle in Spanish and *hornillo* is a small oven. The *pava hornillo* was invented in Perú in the eighteenth century and it was used to have hot water nearby. The kettle has a receptacle for the ember and an ingenuous system of pipes to keep the ember glowing.

Brazilian Mate

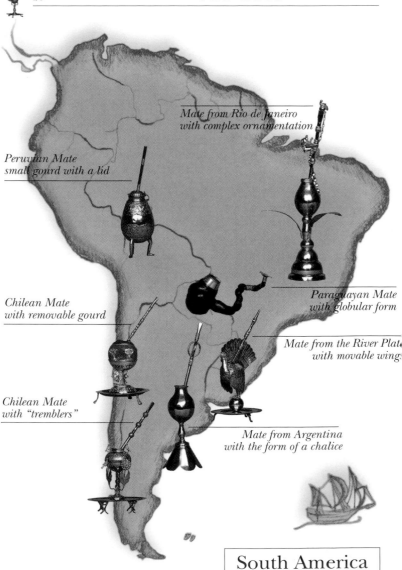

Mate from Rio de Janeiro
with complex ornamentation

Peruvian Mate
small gourd with a lid

Chilean Mate
with removable gourd

Paraguayan Mate
with globular form

Mate from the River Plate
with movable wings

Chilean Mate
with "tremblers"

Mate from Argentina
with the form of a chalice

South America

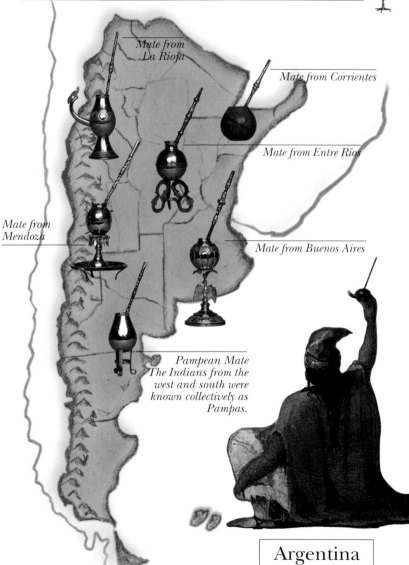

Mate from La Rioja

Mate from Corrientes

Mate from Entre Ríos

Mate from Mendoza

Mate from Buenos Aires

Pampean Mate
The Indians from the west and south were known collectively as Pampas.

Argentina

How to Brew Mate

Mate is usually drunk without sugar and it is called mate cimarrón *or* cimarrón, *(cimarrón was the name given to the cattle that ran wild). Some people, especially women, drink mate with sugar, adding a spoonful of sugar every two brewings.*
Mate can also be brewed with cold water (tereré) *or with milk and sugar* (mate misqui). *It can be flavoured with mint or lemon or orange peel. Some people even add cinnamon.*

Mate from Buenos Aires
The bombilla has been divided at the top to cool the mate.

Brewing mate needs time and an atmosphere of peace and tranquility, two ingredients that have become pretty scarce nowadays. A mate (the gourd) half full of *yerba* (the leaves) and a *bombilla* (the tube with the strainer) are also needed. The *cebador* (the person in charge of preparing the mate, the master of ceremonies) will then put his wet hand on the mate and shake it so that the powder, which comes with the *yerba*, will stick to his hand and so prevent the *bombilla* from getting blocked.

This is the moment in which the *bombilla* has to be stuck into the mate and the water poured into it in such a way, that it has to glide along the *bombilla*, not wetting the *yerba* at the top. A difficult task. Some *cebadores* pour the water before sticking in the *bombilla*. They leave the *yerba* to swell and then they put the *bombilla* in. Those who put the *bombilla* in before the water usually start the procedure by pouring a small amount of cold water.

The water should always be hot but not boiling. Boiling water will "stun" the mate. Once the mate is prepared, the *bombilla* should not be moved because one runs the risk of blocking it.

The first mate brewed is called "the fool's mate", and it is drunk by the *cebador*.

Water is added again and again, wetting the *yerba* upwards.

Cebar means exactly that, maintain or feed the mate. After some time, depending on the ability of the *cebador*, the *yerba* loses its flavour, it is "washed" and the first symptom is the absence of froth, the distinctive characteristic of a good mate. When the *yerba* is washed, the mate is emptied and the procedure of brewing starts again from the very beginning. Mate has to be brewed by only one person. When the *cebador* gets tired, he just "hangs the mate" and everybody stops drinking.

If you happen to say *gracias*, (thank you), when offered a mate, then the *cebador* will understand that you do not want to drink or you want to stop drinking. Mate can also be drunk like tea in a cup, then it is called "mate cocido", meaning cooked or boiled mate.

R. A. Q. Monvoisin (1790-1870) Soldier of Rosas

The Virtues of Yerba

Mate from Buenos Aires

"Most people who drink mate every day have a blooming complexion", Juan Sanchez Labrador, S. J. Paraguay Natural.

Mate is considered a stimulating drink. It not only stimulates the nervous system and the circulation but it is an excellent regulator of the digestive system.

It contributes to the storage of phosphorus, one of the most important mineral constituents needed for cellular activity.

F. Paillet (1880-1967) Immigrants drinking Mate

Furthermore it has an important beneficial action on those portions of the brain responsible for the memory, and it helps people to recover from mental fatigue.

A less frequent use of *yerba mate* is explained by Father Sánchez Labrador in his famous book *Paraguay Natural*. He writes: "If yerba is left in water to ferment or if (to accelerate the process) the leaves are cooked in water and then afterwards they are pressed, one can get a very good black ink used for writing." And he adds that this ink "can also be used as an excellent dye."

Recipes

On rainy days, in the country, when nothing can be done except stay at home, *tortas fritas* (fritters), or *pastelitos de dulce de membrillo* (quince tarts) are prepared and eaten while drinking mate.

Pampean Mate

Tortas Fritas (Fritters)
Ingredients: 400 gr flour
           150 gr fat
           1 tsp salt dissolved in water
           water
           sugar

Put the flour onto a working surface. Make a well in the centre and add the fat and the salt. Mix them together adding the necessary amount of water so as to form a smooth dough. Knead well and then roll out and cut in rounds which should not be thicker than ½ cm. Prick them well and fry them in hot fat, turning them to brown evenly.

Mate from Mendoza

C. Morel
(1813-1894)

Young Girl from Lima

Mate from La Rioja

Mate from Entre Rios

J. L. Camaña
(1795-1877)
Playing Mus

Pastelitos (Quince Tarts)
Ingredients: ½ kg flour
            1 tsp sugar
            pinch of salt
            150 gr butter
            1 cup of milk
            ½ kg quince jam
            fat

Put the flour, the sugar and the salt onto the working surface. Make a well in the centre and add milk and 100 gr butter. Mix rapidly and leave the pastry covered to rest for half an hour. Roll out and put butter on one half of the pastry and enclose it by folding over the other pastry half. Repeat the procedure 4 times. Roll out again and cut squares of 6 cm, put a spoonful of quince jam in the centre and cover it with another square, wetting the sides with water so that they stick together. Seal the edges by pressing. Fry the tarts in hot fat, bathing them constantly to brown evenly.

Travellers

Many visitors to Argentina, especially English speaking travellers, have written interesting reports of their long voyages in Argentina and they have invariably described the mate ceremony. Here are some excerpts:

South American Sketches, by Thomas Woodbine Hinchliff, London, 1863

"In addition to the shops there are several excellent markets, where not only meat and bread, but quantities of beautiful living birds, skins, feathers, and all kinds of country curiosities, are to be found: the famous yerba, or Paraguay tea, made from the leaves of a species of ilex in that luxuriant climate, is sold in vast quantities, to make the favourite drink of the country; and another staple commodity is a small gourd, with the stem for a handle, which forms the teapot, or mate, from which it is imbibed, like a sherry-cobbler, the *bombilla*, or silver tube, being put into the mate before the hot water is applied. This is an almost universal beverage among both sexes and all classes of the community and seems to be equally acceptable at any time of day or night, either in town or country … Up the country in every shepherd's hut where a traveller stops to rest himself and his horse, the good woman of the house instantly retires to make mate for the new visitor, who would be considered something of a barbarian if he declined the delicacy…"

Ernest William White (1881)

"…the Gaucho, possessing few wants and poor in the midst of inexhaustible riches, is the child of un-concern; with food or without, with shelter or not, a paper cigar, a little mate (Para-guayan tea), one meal a day of meat cooked in the open air without bread or vegetables, and his guitar at night, and he rests content: but if you add a Sunday suit of clothes with silver-mounted trappings for his horse, his pride and delight are unbounded, and as he curvets over the plain, having attained the summit of his ambition, no more vivid picture of human self-satisfaction could be presented."

Around and About South America, Twenty Months of Quest and Query by Frank Vincent, New York, 1889.

Mate from de River Plate

"*Mate* and cigarettes are as ubiquitous here as coffee and pipes in the Levant. *Mate* is taken the first thing in the morning, and again about the middle of the afternoon, regularly. Then, besides, whenever you call upon a person, at any time of day or evening, *mate* is generally served as a delicate attention, whether your visit is of business or friendship."

To the River Plate and Back by W. J. Holland, London, 1913

Porcelain Mate Made in Germany

"...and the water which has been heated almost to the boiling-point is poured into the gourd, and after a few seconds the drink is ready to be drawn up into the mouth through the tube. From time to time as the tea is exhausted more hot water may be supplied, and the process of imbibition goes on. In the rural districts the drinking of mate is universal among the creoles. The gourd is passed from hand to hand, and each one who receives it, takes a draught from the *bombilla*, which must not be unduly disturbed, as it is thought that the stirring of the mixture impairs its quality. The fear of the deadly microbe has only recently

been implanted in the minds of men, and has not yet thoroughly invaded the remoter districts of South America.

To those who possess this wholesome horror, the custom of passing the bombilla from mouth to mouth does not commend itself…"

A. D'Hastrel
(1805-1875)
The Tristes Singer
(Tristes are sad songs)

C. Morel
(1813-1894)
An Hour Before Departure

J. M. Blanes
(1830-1901)
The Red Chiripá

"The drinking of mate does not obtrude itself upon the eye in Buenos Aires and other large cities, where the population is largely of foreign origin, but among the inhabitants of smaller towns and villages, where the foreign influence is not strong, it is almost universal, and a great deal of time is reported to be wasted in mate-drinking, which goes on at all hours."

Gleanings and Remarks by Major Alexander Gillespie, London, 1818

C. Morel
(1813-1894)

"So long as their *matesitos* and *papels* were issued regularly, the *blandengo* (*blan-dengue*, a soldier) felt himself independent. The former allowance consisted in a certain weight of the herb of Paraguay, which is taken when very thirsty, or before meals, by the *peons* (a *peon* is an agricultural labourer) in these parts of South America, in a decoction from warm, if it can be had, or cold water without sugar. The operation is completed in the first instance within a minute, and in the last requires two, for if a longer time, the liquor assumes a dark colour, which is reckoned less wholesome.

Every one carries a small bladder to hold it, and a pouch for his paper *segars*, with a steel and flint to raise a fire for his provisions and pipe. Thus equipped, and with his horse and lasso to supply hunger, the soldier will keep the field for months, killing an ox when wanted, turning off his animal when tired, and taking another at will. As chocolate was scarce, and tea could not be had, we adopted the vulgar fashion of mate to breakfast. It grows upon a tree of the evergreen oak class, about the size of a small pear, and prefers a marshy soil … At first it was unpleasant from its bitterness, but we latterly preferred it to any beverage, and its happy effects as a stomachic medicine were fully ascertained. The best portions of it are the powdered particles, the rest being like cut hay and less strong. If East India monopoly would allow of its importation, it would soon obtain general consumption amongst the lower orders, as healthful nourishing substitute for tea, and I doubt not the apothecary might be much indebted to its virtues."

Illustration by W. J. Holland

Book Cover W. J. Holland, 1913

Index

F. Paucke, S. J., (1719-1779), Canes that grow in the jungle

Establecimiento Las Marías: Aerial view of yerba mate plantations

Establecimiento Orgánico Kraus: Morning dew on yerba leaves.

*"From central Brazil to Patagonia, mate is the beverage of choice for stimulation, nutrition and social gatherings.
A growing number of health-conscious folks in Europe, Asia and North America enjoy mate as an alternative to coffee and black tea."*

Joseph Chermesino

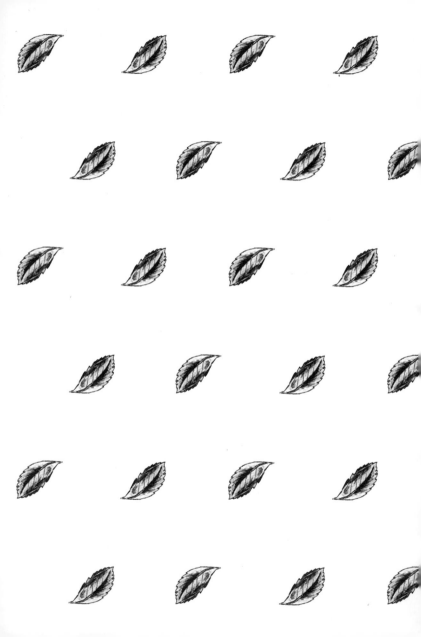